THE SOLUTION OF CHOICE

Four good ideas that neutralized Western Christianity

Marcus Warner | Jim Wilder

The Solution of Choice: Four good ideas that neutralized Western Christianity

© 2018 E. James Wilder and Marcus Warner

All rights reserved. No portion of this book may be reproduced, stored in a retrieval system, or transmitted in any form or by any means—electronic, mechanical, photocopy, recording, scanning, or other—except for brief quotations in critical reviews or articles, without the prior written permission of the publisher.

Published by Deeper Walk International

First Printing April, 2018 / Printed in the United States of America

ISBN: 978-1-62890-493-2

Bible quotations translated by Marcus Warner unless otherwise noted.

Deeper Walk International
13295 Illinois St. #223
Carmel, Indiana 46032

www.DeeperWalkInternational.org

Table of Contents

About the Authors 5

Chapter One – The Enlightenment Shift . . 9

Chapter Two – A Skewed Model 19

Chapter Three – Truth 29

Chapter Four – Choice 35

Chapter Five – Power 49

Chapter Six – Tolerance 57

Chapter Seven – The *Hesed* Solution 67

Author Biographies 81

About the Authors

Between their two families, Dr. Marcus Warner (and his wife Brenda) and Dr. Jim Wilder (and his wife Kitty) have covered much of the Christian world. They have directly seen the church in action in Austria, Brazil, Cambodia, Canada, Chile, Colombia, Costa Rica, Ecuador, France, Germany, Himalayas, Hungary, India, Ireland, Mexico, Netherlands, Nicaragua, Nigeria, Poland, Romania, South Korea, South Sudan, Spain, Sri Lanka, Switzerland, Thailand, Ukraine, and the USA.

Between these two authors, they have spoken to students and faculty at Talbot Seminary, Fuller Seminary, Trinity Evangelical Divinity School, Moody Bible Institute, Bethel College, Tyndale Seminary, Presbyterian Seminary of Mexico City, St John Vianney Seminary, Duke Divinity School, Biola University, Point Loma University, Montreat College, and Payap University.

Dr. Warner has taught Old Testament and Theology at Bethel College in Mishawaka, Indiana (as well as adjunct roles for Huntington University, Trinity College, and Trinity Evangelical Divinity School). He served on the staffs of a Missionary Church, an Evangelical Free Church, and spent seven years as senior pastor of a non-denominational church in Carmel, Indiana. Today, Marcus serves as the president of Deeper Walk International, a ministry founded by the author Mark I. Bubeck.

Their associations with Christian leaders include lunches and dinners with Henry Blackaby, John Eldredge, Erwin Lutzer, Walter Martin, Jack Wyrtzen and a host of pastors and non-profit leaders; group cookout at the home of Dr. Billy Graham, a longtime friendship with Dr. Dallas and Jane Willard, attending church with Dr. James Dobson and speaking to his staff, consulting with the church where John McArthur grew up, being asked to teach psychology at his Master's College, working with program developers at Jack Hayford's The Church on the Way, mixing with Dr. Ralph Winter and the US Center for World Mission, speaking next to Dr. Neil Anderson, Dr. George Bebawi, Dr. C. Fred Dickason, Dr. Charles Kraft, Dr. Celestin Musakura, Dr. Ed Murphy, Dr. John Perkins, Fr. Ubald Rugirangoga, Dr. Ed Smith, and many more.

The authors have worked with Armenian, Anglican, Assemblies of God, Baptist, Brethren, Eastern Rite and Roman Catholic, Christian Community Development (CCDA), Congregational, Coptic, Foursquare, Lutheran, Mennonite, Messianic, Methodist, Moody Church, Navigators, "Plain People" (from Amish and other groups), Reformed, Salvation Army, SIM, Verbo, Vineyard, Voice of the Martyrs, Willow Creek Prison Ministry, Wycliffe, YWAM, and more.

Jim's brother Timothy started in medieval studies and did graduate work in theology with a particular interest in Reformed Theology and advanced study in philosophy. Decades of discussion between the two brothers has influenced the thought in this booklet.

The authors represent an unusually wide and deep exposure to Christian faith, theology, and practice around the world. It is with this perspective that the two have lovingly taken a second look at the lack of character transformation in the Western church, how we got where we are, and how we need to change course to correct the situation.

1: The Enlightenment Shift

Nearly five hundred years ago, the church made a sharp left turn in response to the Enlightenment. It is a shift from which we have never fully recovered. This shift created a skewed paradigm that has left the church offering solutions for character change that have not worked. There are far too many Christians living as if real character change will only happen on the other side of eternity. But what if Christ-likeness was meant to be a reality in this life? Is it really necessary for so many Christians to feel like the best they can do is hold on until they die?

We will see how four great Enlightenment ideas have neutralized the church and how something we all know but rarely understand can bring us transformed lives.

What's the Enlightenment got to do with it?

The scientific revolution started a philosophical earthquake that shook Western culture to its very foundations. Pioneers like Galileo and Copernicus proved mathematically that the earth was going around the sun. This may not seem like a big deal, but it was a blow that changed Western civilization forever.

The problem wasn't that they had made a new discovery. The problem was that they had proved the church was wrong about something. The official catechism of the church taught that the sun went around a fixed earth. But if the church was wrong about this, how could you trust them to be right about anything else?

Philosophers were quick to grasp this dilemma. What if the theology of the Dark Ages was as wrong about the psychology of humans and how humans worked as it had been about the sun and the planets? If the church was not the final arbiter of what was true and false—of what was right and wrong—a whole new world of possibilities emerged.

It felt to many that culture was moving from the Dark Ages to an age of Enlightenment, in which science and philosophy would guide us to truth, rather than the church. The church fought back, however, producing a hot debate about the psychology of human beings and how this impacted salvation. A fierce battle began within the church to determine what made a human become a child of God: was it truth in the intellect, a choice by the will, the heart and emotions, or something else?

Truth - the foundation of unity or division?

The issue of intellectual truth was central to Enlightenment philosophy. Free thinkers wanted to uncover how we know what is true and how much truth is actually knowable. Authors like Descartes, Locke, Hume, and Kant explored the role and limits of reason and experience in uncovering indisputably true facts. For such thinkers, what the Church taught about reality was simply irrelevant to their pursuits. Christianity and philosophy quickly developed an adversarial relationship.

In response to the Enlightenment focus on truth, the church basically said, "We can be as rational as you," and set about proving that Christians were both reasonable and right.

This shift was subtle but profound.

In response to Enlightenment philosophy, truth became the central issue in the Christian faith. Calvin stated that the human soul had both understanding and will, but the understanding "is our most excellent part; it holds primacy in the life of man, is the seat of reason, presides over the will, and restrains vicious desires."[1]

Eventually, the ability to intelligently articulate what one believed to be true and why one believed it became the most important quality of a Christian leader. We sent pastors to seminaries and colleges to train them in right belief and the best defenses of those right beliefs. The model of transformation looked like this.

God + Reason = Transformation

You would think all this focus on truth would lead to a golden age of Christian maturity, but we all know that didn't happen. In fact, the more we focused on truth and being right, the more divisions became necessary. Denominations split over who was right. Churches split over small differences in thought and interpretation. Because truth was the foundation of ev-

---

[1] John Calvin, *Commentary on Romans*, translated R. Mackenzie (Grand Rapids, MI: William B. Eerdmans, 1973), page 265.

erything else, we had to keep those who were "most right" separated from those who were "less right."

Sadly, being right didn't produce life change. There were many leaders who believed all the right things and knew all the right answers but who didn't seem any closer to mastering the art of godly living. The same was true of the people they were trying to lead. Something more than "being right" was needed in order to experience real transformation into Christ-like character.

Choice - the key to transformation?

As the debate about how the human mind operates continued to develop, a second wave of Enlightenment philosophers argued that whether one believed the truth made little difference until one made a choice. A movement emerged among Enlightenment thinkers called Voluntarism (from the Latin word for "will" - *voluntas*).

Man's freedom (from God) to be whatever he wanted to be was a celebrated virtue in Enlightenment circles. Thomas Hobbes pushed the discussion of the will into theological circles by making God a determinist and mocking free will.

The fight was now on for the church to prove that God and human choice fit together somehow in God's psychology. The big problem was the conflict between God having a will and people having a will. How did this work? The discussion over human and divine will has dominated theology for centuries.

Puritan leaders like William Ames infused voluntarist perspectives into American seminaries. "The will is the principle and the first cause of all humane operation," therefore, "it follows that the first and proper subject of theology is the will," Ames stated.[2]

Jonathan Edwards became one of the most influential voices in the development of American Christianity through his writings on the will. Edwards and other voluntarists believed the will was influenced by "affections" and not intellectual reason alone. "Because he was dealing with the most fundamental idea of his community, Jonathan Edwards used *Freedom of the Will* to give reason to his own ideal of human community."[3] The result of this reaction to Enlightenment and Voluntarist philosophies was a model of transformation that looked like this.

God + Choice = Transformation

Voluntarist philosophers and theologians emphasized free will and human choice as the most profound means of life change. It certainly makes sense. Our choices clearly have consequences. Soon, discipline and right choices were central to living the Christian life successfully. The combination of being right and making right choices were heralded by the church as the keys to life change. There is a logic to this that is completely understandable. Believing the truth and making good choices certainly don't work against life change.

---

2 William Ames, *The Marrow of Theology*, translated John D. Eusden, 10.
3 Allen C. Guelzo, *Edwards on the Will,* (Middletown, CN: Wesleyan University Press, 1989) page 15.

But if this model is so great, one has to wonder, why has it produced such poor fruit?

This model has become so engrained in our thinking that we rarely question it. Few pastors or leaders stop to wonder if there could be a better way to develop Christ-like disciples. As a result, most discipleship and most counseling services offered by the church are built on providing more truth and better choices. Good information should lead to good choices, right? Yet, we all know this doesn't work.

Therefore, as we pointed out in *Rare Leadership*, this model always leads to the need for a strong accountability system. In fact, most of us simply take for granted that there is no life change without strong accountability.

This Enlightenment-driven model has been driving the solutions to our problems for over 400 years. As one TV psychologist likes to ask, "How's that working for ya?" Perhaps it is time to question the model.

Power - the secret weapon of the church?

Arthur Schopenhauer was one philosopher who put his money on the will, but his disciple Friedrich Nietzsche went further. Nietzsche argued that the will was only significant if it led to the power to take action and get results.

This "will to power" explained human psychology and the desire for achievement, ambition, and best of life. Alfred Adler built a psychology system out of this power drive. Even the Nazi government took a ride on their version of this philosophy.

Christians found themselves in a world talking about power. Truth, information, and even good choices were not producing transformation in many lives.

So, many Christians came to the conclusion that what must be missing from the gospel being preached was power. The Holy Spirit would certainly be the place to find more power. They had tried Bible study and detailed doctrinal statements. They had tried to make the right choices and implement systems of accountability, but it left them stagnant. So, they adopted a new model of transformation that looked like this.

Power + Faith = Transformation

This was certainly my story (Marcus). I grew up reading and memorizing Scripture. I began teaching the Bible in ninth grade (and I've never quit). But I found myself at a crossroads during seminary. I knew more about the Bible and right belief than most Christians I knew. I worked hard at being a good Christian. But I was depressed. The solution of choice (choosing to do what I knew to be right) wasn't getting the job done. In my frustration, I figured my problem was that I didn't speak in tongues, and I became fascinated with those who did. It made sense that my Christianity didn't work because it lacked power.

THE SOLUTION OF CHOICE WASN'T GETTING THE JOB DONE.

However, I soon became disillusioned by the fact that most of the people I knew who were operating in the power of the Spirit weren't any more mature than I was.

In fact, in many cases, I found I was the most stable person in the room. One church I attended where spiritual power was celebrated as the key to the Christian life was, quite frankly, a mess. The pastor routinely taught completely contradictory ideas in the same sermon, and no one seemed to notice.

I believe in the power of the Spirit and have seen hundreds of demons evicted from people, experienced the miraculous, and heard the Spirit's voice, but none of these things generated life change on their own.

Such experiences are encouraging and even exciting, but spiritual power is not the foundation on which the Christian faith is built, and it does not necessarily produce character or build virtue. There are enough examples of fallen leaders with "powerful" anointings to make that case.

I began my journey hoping that spiritual power was the secret weapon of the church and was left looking for something more.

Tolerance - the new solution?

If believing right things, making right choices, and experiencing spiritual power are not enough to produce life change, what is left? The new point of emphasis in the church today is tolerance. Yet, once again, the church is simply following culture on this point.

- When the Enlightenment made truth the most important part of being human, the church responded by making truth the foundation of the faith.

- When Voluntarism argued that choices were the key to life change, the church agreed and tried offering better choices.

- When Modernism turned to power as the central issue in life, the church soon followed once again.

Today, as postmodernism holds sway, the church has agreed with the philosophers that *tolerance* is the highest virtue, and agreed that there are some things you just can't change.

Culture believes people are born a certain way and there is nothing you can do about it, and the church is following. Therefore, the church seems to believe we need to accept and embrace everyone as they are *without any expectation of change.*

Tolerance, in the sense of loving your enemies, is a Christian virtue. But tolerance without any expectation of change is not Christian. It is the logical result of a failed system anchored in Enlightenment and Voluntarist ideas.

This sort of tolerance is merely waving the white flag of surrender and saying, "The church has nothing to offer capable of producing transformation, so let's just accept the fact and get on with life."

The model of transformation in too many churches today looks like this:

WE DON'T REALLY EXPECT TRANSFORMATION.

Conclusion

The solutions for life change traditionally offered by the church have failed. It is time for a new solution. To get to that solution, we need to understand why the old model failed to produce solutions that really work. In the end, our goal is to urge the church to embrace a new model—a deeply biblical model—that offers a new set of solutions for producing transformation. Follow along as we go a little deeper.

2: Skewed Models

The premise of this book is that the church has been offering limited and often flawed solutions to those who come to us for help, because we have been operating out of a flawed model. When your paradigm is skewed, your answers get skewed. We can see this clearly in the history of medicine.

Today, it is common for doctors to wear white lab coats that proclaim to all how committed they are to maintaining a sterile environment. But that wasn't always the case. There was a day when doctors wore black lab coats. The dark color helped hide the splattered blood that was soaked into them. When people first began to suggest that surgeons wash their hands and clean their instruments between operations, they were met with scorn. "Why waste valuable time washing hands? Patients are dying. It would be immoral to waste even a few minutes tending to our own desire for cleanliness!"

Without the right model—one that understood the problem of bacteria and germs—they couldn't see the solution. In fact, they ridiculed the solution. Sadly, it is often the same way with the church.

Discipleship without character change

Most serious Christians wonder why we are not more changed by our faith.

Many of us settle into a routine of going to church that is comfortable but not particularly transformative. This may be because comfort and transformation have little to do with each other. It takes a crisis before most people change.

It is a common saying in support group ministries that people don't do something about their addictions until the pain being caused by their addiction is greater than the pain they are trying to avoid. Most of us never question the quality of our discipleship experience until crisis and pain reveal what is lacking.

It doesn't occur to many who attend church that there is any problem with the way they are being discipled until they have a crisis they can't handle. When they get overwhelmed by panic attacks, and reading Bible verses about faith doesn't make them stop, they realize they need something more than what they have. When Christians vow to quit the porn habit they've been hiding but can't seem to find the will power to stop for more than a week or two, they wonder why their Christianity isn't working. When a loved one dies, when chronic pain enters their world, when disaster of any kind hits, many of us discover that our approach to Christianity is lacking something crucial. We just aren't quite sure what it is.

> **MOST OF US NEVER QUESTION THE QUALITY OF OUR DISCIPLESHIP UNTIL CRISIS AND PAIN REVEAL WHAT IS LACKING.**

Character change and irrelevance

When it comes to character change, many of the solutions offered by the church don't seem to be very effective. Because our solutions are not making us more godly, more loving, more joyful, better able to endure suffering or to grow in self-discipline, the message is becoming irrelevant to church members. Parents are becoming irrelevant to children. And the church is becoming irrelevant to society.

When Neil Anderson first developed *The Steps to Freedom in Christ*, he was teaching at Talbot seminary. Part of his motivation in developing this tool was the desire to stop sending so many young men into ministry with obvious defects in their character. Far too many of them were in bondage to bitterness, sexual desire, family dysfunction, and habitual sin. *The Steps* were developed to help resolve some of the most common problems that kept these future pastors in spiritual bondage, because the education they had received had done nothing to address them.

Many students graduate seminary without ever experiencing a meaningful relationship with a professor. One of the reasons for this may be explained by an insight from Marcus's father, Timothy Warner. When he was tasked by Trinity Evangelical Divinity School to oversee their accreditation renewal in the 1980s, he sent out a survey to the faculty.

One of the questions asked, "Do you see your job as discipling students or teaching your discipline?" About 50% of the faculty saw themselves as discipling the students. What was particularly telling, however, was that in the Bible and theology departments 100% said their job was to teach their discipline. Is it any surprise, therefore, that most seminary graduates feel unprepared for ministry and often struggle with character problems? They are well educated messes without any deeply meaningful relationships.

This following testimony was submitted by a student at a prominent Evangelical seminary. It expresses an experience that can be echoed by thousands of other Christians.

> I have never been discipled, and I have been a Christian for 20 years. Because of not knowing who I am in Christ, I did not know how to walk according to the Spirit. Therefore, I have been living my life according to the flesh while gaining a lot of head knowledge about the Bible and God. . . .
> I have struggled so long because of my weakness to say no to myself, and I have really been ineffective for Christ. I was always told by those that I opened up to what to do, but it never had any power in my life. I know a lot of theology, and I know everything I should do; but I do not bear much fruit, and I do not love others the way God wants me to. I have prayed a long time that God would show me how to get my head knowledge to my heart, and now He has shown me the way. I feel like a baby Christian because I have to start at the basics again, but I will swallow my pride and learn how to reprogram my faulty ways of thinking. I have grown up with a poor self-esteem, self-condemnation, self-hatred, bitterness, rebellion, perfectionism, anxiety and a weak functional faith. . . .

I had needs that I tried to have fulfilled by lust, pornography, eating, acceptance by others, withdrawal, and facades. My life is filled with hurts, and I have responded to them incorrectly. I used to really struggle because of my view of how God views me. By reading a couple of helpful books on God's grace, I have been freed from the mentality of perfectionism for God's acceptance and love. Yet my life is still powerless because of my faulty patterns of thoughts, many of which are strongholds.[4]

When you hear success stories coming from seminary students, it is almost always because of meaningful relationships they formed and community they developed. Students who stay isolated and just get good information don't leave seminary prepared for life much less ministry. But those who make meaningful relationships and get even a little taste of a deeply bonded community nearly always experience a positive shift in their character growth.

Playing "follow the leader" with Enlightenment Culture

Since the days of the Enlightenment, the church has basically been playing a game of "follow the leader." Every time the culture changes, we change. The whole goal of many contemporary churches is to be as much like the culture as possible. This is great for drawing a crowd to hear the gospel. It is not so great for creating life change. In our quest to be culturally relevant, the church has far too often allowed the world to mold us into their own image.

---

[4] This quote is taken from Marcus Warner, *Toward A Deeper Walk* (Deeper Walk: Carmel, 2006) p. 13

Western models of discipleship and ministry preparation have tended to be very intellectual and individual. However, it is not uncommon in other cultures for discipleship to be focused on belonging that creates identity and shapes values. Belonging-based discipleship was the norm in the New Testament church.

For instance, Barnabas brought Saul of Tarsus into the believing community, and belonging was key to his transformation. One-on-one mentoring was not the major factor in Paul's discipling. It was time spent directly with Jesus and the experience of community that he took with him everywhere he went. Paul was no lone ranger. He traveled in a team, he planted communities, he taught people how to make community work. The fanatic who became the apostle Paul understood the power of belonging to transform and put more emphasis on the cross, the Spirit, and community to bring about change than on one-one-one mentoring.

The emphasis on intellect and individuality goes back to the church's response to the Enlightenment. The scientific approach emphasizes causality—how you make things happen. The Enlightenment approach to science says that all things have natural or scientific causes and, therefore, can be controlled to some extent by humans. This paradigm influenced the church in significant ways. We became much more focused on how to make ministry happen through our own efforts, our own reason, and our own choices. We became more focused on measuring results, and character is not easy to measure. As a result, we focused on things that could be measured.

- Knowledge: Have you mastered your lessons?
- Attendance: How many people showed up?
- Conduct: Did you obey the rules? Are you wearing the right clothes? etc.

The Enlightenment influence on truth also led to an emphasis on being right. In response, Christians made being right more important than being in relationship. We became adversarial and arrogant about truth: "We have more truth than you do! We are more right than you are!"

"Salvation" came to be seen as a future destination rather than community now and character change in the present. The key to making sure you arrived at that future destination was to have your ticket in hand, and you got that ticket by believing right things—by believing what was true.

Salvation as a loving attachment to the Savior was replaced by a salvation based on creed.

Once Voluntarism became dominant, the church went along with it, and said, "No one makes better choices than we do. We are not only more right than you, we make better choices than you." What the church did not excel at was keeping relationships bigger than problems.

THE CHURCH DID NOT EXCEL AT KEEPING RELATIONSHIPS BIGGER THAN PROBLEMS.

The situation reminds me of the story of the monk who toured the Vatican with a powerful pope who showed him all the gold and exquisite decorations. The pope said, "No longer do we have to say, 'silver and gold have we none.'" To which the monk replied, "True. But can we still say, 'In the name of Jesus of Nazareth, rise up and walk?'"

In the twentieth century, Western culture turned to fascism and the belief that power could create a new world. After fascism collapsed, we turned to Eastern religion and a different kind of power—the spiritual power of the New Age movement. In response, the church also turned to power. New waves of emphasis on the spiritual power available to Christians came into vogue. Instead of asking, "Who is more right?" the church started asking, "Who has more power?" If you wanted to compliment an activity or a person, the highest praise you could bestow was, "My, wasn't that powerful!"

TOLERANCE AND LOVE ARE NOT THE SAME.

Today, the chief quality admired by the culture is tolerance, and once again the church has followed along. Rather than building discipleship agendas focused on producing people who love the way Christ loved, we are still stuck with agendas focused on truth, choice, power, and now tolerance. But tolerance and love are not the same thing.

Tolerance, as practiced by the culture, is actually the source of quite a bit of hate. If you are not as tolerant as I am, that seems to give me permission to hate you. As Josef Tson said at an ICBC conference in 2002, "The world operates by three principles—deception, hatred, and violence. Deception leads to hatred, and hatred leads to violence."

Lost in Enlightenment packaging

In a post-Christian world where being right has not produced better character and there is no standard for who is right, the power of the Gospel to transform has been lost in Enlightenment packaging. Christianity has been following the culture and letting it impact us, rather than the church impacting the culture. As a result we have often missed out on the chance to bring our message to them.

3: Truth

In a thought-provoking TED talk, psychiatrist and brain science specialist, Iain McGilchrist dismissed the commonly held idea that the right side of the brain is where we do emotion and the left side of the brain is where we do reason.[5] Rather, both sides of the brain are essential to both emotion and reason.

The two hemispheres of the brain are radically different, but not in that way. They look at and interact with the world in two completely different ways, giving us two completely different versions of reality. The left brain is designed to focus. It looks at a very limited part of the world and analyzes it. However, that analysis will be lifeless and empty because the left brain does not experience reality relationally. It experiences life analytically. It *thinks* about relationships. It doesn't *do* relationships.

The left brain looks for problems to solve and ways to grasp what is going on in the world around it so it can solve those problems. When the left brain is operating without much right brain input, you get a non-relational, problem-focused approach to living in which culture prioritizes "the virtual over the real (we would rather watch a sit-com about relationships than experience relationships); the technical becomes important (we are more comfortable amassing data and analyz-

---
5   https://www.ted.com/talks/iain_mcgilchrist_the_divided_brain

ing how life works than living), and bureaucracy flourishes (because we see people like problems to solve rather than humans to help)."⁶

Left-brain dominated people and left-brain dominated cultures tend to isolate themselves from anything that could challenge their perspectives and bring about real change. The left brain desires a perfectly explainable world, and new perspectives and people make that impossible, so it likes to live in avoidance.

> WE HAVE A PROBLEM-FOCUSED, ANALYTICAL CHURCH THAT IS GOOD AT DOING TASKS AND TALKING ABOUT IDEAS.

The left brain is not evil, nor is it unimportant, but it is less vital to living as a human being than the right brain. A quote often attributed to Einstein puts it this way, "The intuitive mind is a sacred gift, and the rational mind is a faithful servant. We live in a society that honors the servant, but has forgotten the gift."⁷ This is a good way to look at it. People and cultures who cultivate and celebrate the qualities of life that are dominant in the right brain are more relational, more engaged, and more attuned to the experiences of life.

> WHAT WE HAVE MISSED IS A CHURCH THAT EXCELS AT EMPATHY, COMPASSION, FORMING DEEP BONDS, AND LOVING OUR ENEMIES.

---

6   The quote is from Iain McGilchrist's TEDS talk. The words in parentheses are editorial comments.

7   According to http://quoteinvestigator.com/2013/09/18/intuitive-mind this quote has been posted across social media as coming from Einstein, but it seems to be an altered summary based on a book about Einstein by Bob Samples in 1976 called *The Metaphoric Mind: A Celebration of Creative Consciousness.*

Since the days of the Enlightenment we have lived in an increasingly left-brain dominated world of virtual reality, redundant information, and relational isolation. Sadly, the church has simply followed along, unable to see what we have lost in our abandonment of all God intended the right brain to do. Therefore, we have a problem-focused, analytical church that is good at doing tasks and talking about ideas. What we have missed is a church that excels at empathy, compassion, forming deep bonds, and loving our enemies.

Truth is a person

We think of truth as a proposition. Rational truth is all about concepts and logic. However, there is a different kind of truth than the left-brain, propositional truth we are used to. To put it another way, there is left-brain knowing and right-brain knowing. The left brain views truth as a proposition to be analyzed. The right brain views truth as a reality to experience.

Have you ever been in a relationship in which you were so caught up in analyzing where you stood in that relationship, you weren't free to enjoy it? Your left brain was so focused on defining the relationship, your right brain rarely got around to just enjoying the person. In the same way, the left brain looks at truth as a lifeless thing to be analyzed, organized, and systemized into a perfectly operating machine. Your right brain looks at truth as the key to living life more fully. It doesn't put truth

> GOD WANTS US TO KNOW HIM, NOT IN A PROPOSITIONAL WAY, BUT IN A RELATIONAL WAY.

into words (that is the left brain's job). It experiences truth through relationship and engagement with the world around it.

God wants us to know Him, not in a propositional way, but in a relational way. This is the core concept in the Hebrew word *yada*. It refers to the knowledge of experience and relationship rather than the lifeless knowledge of concepts. I may learn true, lifeless facts about someone as I get to know them, but that is not the goal of *yada*. *Yada* is the knowledge that comes from right-brain relational attachment rather than left-brain intellectual assessment.

Repackaging and reducing truth

The Enlightenment created a huge cultural shift to the left side of the brain. In response to this shift, the Christian church repackaged its message in a series of left-brain friendly, Enlightenment-approved insights. This repackaging of the faith into a set of ideas to be believed (and intellectually defended), actually led to a disastrous reduction in the truth of what it meant to be Christian.

By following the lead of Enlightenment philosophers, the Christian church ended up reducing its understanding of truth from the full right-brain, relational experience of Jesus and His kingdom, to a caricature of the truth embodied in feeble, left-brain propositions and ideas. As a result, we took the glorious reality of all that Jesus came to reveal and reduced it to a series of theological statements to which agreement was required. In repackaging Christianity to be acceptable to Enlightenment thinkers, we lost something essential to the Christian faith. We lost truth as a relational encounter.

We also lost the initiative in the culture war. Enlightenment thinkers became the initiators. We became the responders. By accepting the idea that rational truth is the foundation of life, the church changed. It started playing by the Enlightenment's rules rather than by the Kingdom rules Jesus taught us to follow.

Consider some of the ways the Enlightenment changed the church.

- The Enlightenment told us the ability to reason is what makes us human. In response, the church focused more and more on propositional truth and systematic theology. But we have to ask, "Does knowing the best theology really produce the best Christian character?"

- Voluntarism told us we are defined by the choices we make and that the will is core to being human. In response, the church told people that making better choices would make them better Christians. But we have to ask, "Does knowing what we should do effectively change our habits?"

We have to ask, "Have church splits over doctrine produced higher quality Christians than we had before?" "Have divisions over codes of behavior produced more loving followers of Christ?" If being right and making right choices hasn't produced a higher quality of Christian, could it be that the model is defective? Could it be that we let the Enlightenment rather than the Kingdom determine the way we live out our faith?

Conclusion

Winning the "I am right" argument is not the way to develop the character of Christ. As we have all too often seen, it is possible to be very right, but not very relational.

4: CHOICE

How many times have we heard that *sins* are bad choices, *salvation* is a decision, and *character change* is a matter of making better choices?

How many Christian books have told us that love, joy (and most other virtues) are choices we need to make? Haven't we been told we can be anything we choose to be?

Whether we are listening to the latest self-help guru or the newest plan for evangelism, you can be sure it will involve spreading important truth and making good choices. This view of reality is so deeply engrained in our minds we cannot imagine a different way to think. It almost seems bizarre to question the truth of this Enlightenment understanding of human nature.

But it was not always this way.

The Enlightenment's two escape routes

Enlightenment thinkers were not eager to have God's moral rules govern behavior, so they developed two primary escape routes. The first escape from God was **determinism**.

This approach said we are creatures of drives, instincts, passions, affections, chemistry, and energy whose actions are simply a result of the laws of nature. Determinism entered theological discussions forcefully when Thomas Hobbes published *Leviathan* in 1651. The conviction that humans had no real free will entered the realm of psychology in 1971 when the behaviorist B.F. Skinner wrote *Beyond Freedom and Dignity.* He was still arguing that humans' choices were determined by natural forces beyond their control.

The second Enlightenment escape from God's control was a view known as **indeterminism**. Thinkers like Descartes and William James developed the idea that a free human will was central to personal growth and life change. They made choice and chance the primary forces that shaped human behavior. As philosophical indeterminism grew in popularity, it spawned more than twenty schools of thought.

In the heat of this discussion, both church leaders and Enlightenment philosophers became convinced that the secret to the human soul lay in how the will worked. Within the church, discussions about the will centered on salvation—but was it God's will (Calvin) or human will (Arminius) that mattered?

Western minds of every kind, both secular and religious, came to think that the will (or lack of it) was the key to the human soul. Questions about the human will proved much harder to settle than questions about the operation of the solar system.

Only recently have advances in science made it possible to see how the brain really works and understand that the medieval concept of "the will" as a single faculty of the human soul was misguided.

Medieval roots of "the will"

Medieval scholastics spent a lot of time debating human psychology. They divided humans into a set of faculties that included the body, emotions, reason, and will. Some of the most profound thinkers of the era (like Thomas Aquinas) determined that of all the human "faculties" only the will played any part in salvation. Without the will, it was believed, the body and emotions produced impulses and behaviors that ultimately led us down a path to hell.

We haven't really detached ourselves from this medieval model of human nature. Western Christians continue to assume the will is the most important part of being spiritual. While no one believes the medieval psychology anymore, within Western theology the idea of "the will" as a singular entity within the human soul still carries the burden for most of what God wants to do in our lives.

Voluntarist roots of "the will"

The Pilgrims who brought Christianity to the North American colonies were strong believers that right beliefs (the Bible) plus Holy Spirit power led to right choices (the will). Their recipe for transformation was **truth + choices + power** (inner experience) as all that was needed for the Christian life. "The will" was central to their paradigm.

The Pilgrim paradigm grew out of a form of Voluntarist philosophy perhaps best embodied in the work of William Ames. As universities and seminaries were founded throughout Colonial New England, they engaged the Enlightenment writings of philosophers like John Locke and David Hume. In response to such thinkers, Jonathan Edwards produced the massive treatise: *Careful and Strict Inquiry into the Modern Prevailing Notions of Freedom of the Will*. This American statement of theological voluntarism dominated American universities and Christian academics for a century. Although many did not agree with Edwards, the topic of "the will" remained central to the debate.

Time to reassess "the will"

Can we really afford to continue promoting a view of the human will that is rooted in medieval psychology and Voluntarist philosophy? Is this not a path guaranteed to lead us astray?

Given the fact that "the will" as a human faculty was largely a medieval creation, and that the role of the will in both salvation and character change is largely a Voluntarist concept, we have to ask a few questions.

- "Is choice really the only way God works?"

- "Is choice even the main way God creates His character in us?"

- "Is it possible that who we love rather than what we choose might be more central to the solution?"

It is time to reassess the role of "the will" in both salvation and character transformation. To do this, we need to understand what brain science has taught us about choices and "the will" in recent years and reassess the grid through which we have been reading the Scriptures.

A brain-science look at choice

In medieval thought, "the will" was like an engine in the brain that drove the way we live. Brain science has shown that we have **several wills** and that these wills are often in competition with each other. This is why we often experience such intense inner conflict. Our various wills are rooted in our various attachments. They develop through the process of forming attachments and attuning to the world around us. This process ultimately leads to the highest level of brain function where we recognize who our people are and how it is like us to act.

> IS IT POSSIBLE THAT WHO WE LOVE RATHER THAN WHAT WE CHOOSE MIGHT BE MORE CENTRAL TO THE SOLUTION?

- Attachment—Is this personal to me?
- Assessment—Is this good, bad, or scary?
- Attunement—What is happening around me?
- Action/Identity—How it is like me and my people to act in this situation?

All of this activity happens before the part of our brain devoted to conscious thought and making choices even begins to engage in the decision-making process.

In other words, my brain has already ruled out millions of possible choices and decided how it is most like me and my people to act before my left brain ever begins its work of evaluating and making choices. Once the left brain does engage, its primary concern is damage control. It analyzes the options it has been given by the right brain and tries to decide which of those options will create the least amount of damage.

Let's apply this to our Christian experience. Is your Christian faith rooted in attachment or choice? Attachments are the deepest and most anchored part of our brain function. Choices are a function of the most fickle part of our brain. If your brain were a tree, attachments would be the roots, and choices would be up in the leaves somewhere, fluttering back and forth with every fresh breeze that arises. If your Christianity is simply a matter of making one good decision (to receive Jesus) or a series of good decisions, your Christianity will be anchored in your left brain and will function independently of your attachments and your identity. Does that sound very stable?

> **IF YOUR BRAIN WERE A TREE, ATTACHMENTS WOULD BE THE ROOTS, AND CHOICES WOULD BE UP IN THE LEAVES SOMEWHERE.**

God designed the brain to flow from right to left in the way it functions. This means that left-brain decisions do not create right-brain attachments. Nor do they create a right-brain sense of identity or belonging. Brain function doesn't flow that direction. It actually flows the opposite direction.

Who you love (your attachments) form your identity (who are my people and how is it like us to live). Your attachments and identity are far more powerful forces than the moment-by-moment choices you make. When the relational circuits on the right side of your brain are on and firing, you have a much better chance of acting like a Christian than when your circuits are off or malfunctioning.

I (Marcus) experienced this just yesterday. I was tired and something my wife, Brenda, said triggered me, and my relational circuits went off. In this triggered state, my brain was operating in the slow track at the speed of conscious thought, instead of operating in the fast track of my brain that protects relationships. In this condition, I made the bad decision to continue our conversation. You can imagine the results. I said hurtful things and damaged our relationship, and because I wasn't engaged with the attachment center of my brain, I really didn't care. I just wanted to win.

Later, as my circuits got back online, I started feeling like myself and feeling the pain I had caused my wife. Notice that I had at least two wills in conflict in this situation. "The will" in the slow track of my brain that just wanted to win was in conflict with the will in the fast track of my brain that craved relational connection.

What anchors the brain and makes it stable are our attachments. If those attachments are strong and joyful, we get a very healthy and emotionally stable brain. If those attachments are weak or fear-based, my identity is weak and often divided, creating numerous "wills" and greater instability. As a result, my decision making is less grounded and more random.

Left-brain Christianity vs. Whole-brain Christianity

A left-brain approach to Christianity has dominated our culture since the days of the Enlightenment. What we want is a **whole**-brain approach to a Christianity that can transform character. The whole brain starts on the right side of our brain with *who we love* before moving to the left side of the brain with *what we think*.

When left brain functions (like logic, choice, and will) are rooted in right brain functions (like grace, love, and community) they can offer helpful corrections. This is how God designed the brain to function—relationships first, then truth and choice. In this way the whole brain participates in developing character.

The diagram on the next page shows how the fast track and slow track of the brain work together to develop character.

Slow Track	Fast Track
Left Brain (leaves)	Right Brain (roots)
Choice: I use my understanding and belief to solve new problems.	**Grace:** Grace and relational joy must always be expressed.
Beliefs: I check my thinking against what God says is true.	**Love:** Love keeps relationships bigger than problems.
Truth: Truth helps me repent when I forget my true self and people.	**Community:** My people help me live like my true self.

There is nothing wrong with what the left brain does. Making good choices, minimizing negative consequences, and thinking correct thoughts are all good. However, when thoughts become the foundation of Christian character (rather than grace, love, and community) we become performance-oriented and usually legalistic.

A Scriptural look at choice

For hundreds of years, Christianity has been taught as making good choices. It starts with the choice to ask Jesus into your heart and progresses as you learn to make increasingly better and more consistent choices about the way you live. The idea that choice might not be at the heart of Christianity can almost sound heretical. But let's take a closer look.

The concept of human choice is not actually the dominant Scriptural theme most people think it is. When choice is invoked in Scripture, it is generally calling people to remember who their God is and who their people are and to choose to stand with them. Consider two significant passages.

> **THE IDEA THAT CHOICE MIGHT NOT BE AT THE HEART OF CHRISTIANITY CAN ALMOST SOUND HERETICAL. BUT LET'S TAKE A CLOSER LOOK.**

Deuteronomy 30:19-20 (emphasis added)

"I have set before you life and death, blessings and curses. Now **choose life**, so that you and your children may live and that you may **love Yahweh** your God, **listen to His voice**, and **hold fast to Him.** For Yahweh is your life, and He will give you many years in the land He swore to give to your fathers, Abraham, Isaac and Jacob."

Notice the choice they are told to make has to do with relationship—loving, listening, and holding fast to Yahweh. In choosing life, they are choosing Yahweh and relational attachment to Him, "for Yahweh is your life."

> WHEN CHOICE IS INVOKED IN SCRIPTURE, IT IS GENERALLY CALLING PEOPLE TO REMEMBER WHO THEIR GOD IS AND WHO THEIR PEOPLE ARE AND TO CHOOSE TO STAND WITH THEM.

Joshua 24:15 (emphasis added)

"But if serving Yahweh seems undesirable to you, then choose for yourselves this day whom you will serve, whether the gods your ancestors served beyond the Euphrates, or the gods of the Amorites, in whose land you are living. But as for **me and my household, we will serve Yahweh.**"

Again, we see that while choice is the focus, love of Yahweh is the goal. It is a reaffirmation of loyalty that says, "Me and my people are on Yahweh's side, how about you? Are you going to abandon Him after all He has done for you?"

In most texts where the word *choice* is used, God is the one doing the choosing. Interestingly, we do not see God making His choices because of logical reasoning, but because of His attachments. For example, in Deuteronomy 7:7 we read that Yahweh did not choose Israel because they were powerful or numerous, but because they were His.

> **LOVING WELL LEADS TO CHOOSING WELL. CHOOSING WELL MAY NOT LEAD TO LOVE.**

When our choices flow out of loving attachment, we get a completely different experience than when our choices are made without love. Loving well leads to choosing well. Choosing well may not lead to love. Take Jonah for example. Even though he finally chose to go to Nineveh and proclaim its doom, he never loved them. His choice to do the right thing didn't produce attachment.

Does Christianity change character through ideas to be followed?

Due to the influence of the Enlightenment, Christianity has often been reduced to a set of ideas rather than a set of loving relationships. This reduction of Christianity to a left-brain system of ideas and choices is precisely the problem. A Christianity of ideas and choices cannot produce the Christ-like character that loves people well. It will certainly not help us love our enemies. The solution of choice simply does not produce Christ-likeness.

Most Christians come to a crossroads at some point in their journey where they realize they need something more. When that happens, they often look for spiritual power, hoping that more power will help them make better choices. In the next chapter, we will look at the role of power in the Christian faith and explore whether it is the solution so many have claimed it to be.

5: POWER

For 300 years, American Christians have focused on choice as the way to do what God wants us to do. We have increasingly agreed that making choices is the best way to make changes. Now that we have 300 years of practice, we need to ask, "How is focusing on choice (i.e. the will) working?"

- How well is that working with marriage and divorce?
- How well is that working with premarital sex?
- How well is that working with homosexuality and sexual identity?
- How well is that working with your addictions?
- How well is that working with your weight?
- How well is that working with your anxiety?
- How well is that working with your debt?
- How well is that working with loving your enemies?

To this list, we could add anger, porn, depression, church conflicts, family fights, raising teens, and dealing with autism, and ask if choices are changing how you feel and how you react. If you feel lust, but simply choose not to dwell on it, is that the same as developing a character that protects rather than devours? If you feel disgust with your children, but choose to treat them decently anyway, are you not simply practicing damage control? Of course, this is better than not practicing damage control, but it is not the same thing as a changed character.

In the last chapter we saw there are some fundamental problems with a model that focuses on choice (or the will) for character change.

> 1) It started as medieval psychology that is no longer believed by anyone.
>
> 2) It grew in importance as Christianity tried to deal with the disappearing importance of will and choice by Enlightenment thinkers.
>
> 3) It became the focus of the religious/cultural debate at the founding of America and, therefore, is generally found at the core of American Christian theology. (Think Calvinism vs. Arminianism).
>
> 4) The Bible has little focus on choice, and the human will is practically absent from the New Testament.
>
> 5) The idea of a central and single will does not match the brain and how it works.

We have to ask, "Is the goal of the Christian faith to help people manage their character, or to help people change it?"

The Enlightenment shift toward power

Choice (or "the will") failed to explain the soul, and so culture moved on to power. Even within the

Enlightenment, it became clear that having the right ideas and making the right choices did not generate the power to make things happen.

Ironically, as the Voluntarist movement faded in secular circles, it grew stronger in Christian circles. Within secular philosophy, however,

> "IS THE GOAL OF THE CHRISTIAN FAITH TO HELP PEOPLE MANAGE THEIR CHARACTER, OR TO HELP PEOPLE CHANGE IT?"

a shift toward power began to take place. This shift was perhaps best captured by Nietzsche and his concept of "the will to power." What made humans great was not the ability to reason, or the ability to make choices, but the power to make things happen. Nietzsche praised the *ubermensch* (superman) who was able to shape the world through power.

This philosophy fit well with the evolutionary idea of the survival of the fittest and led to an ethic of "might makes right." This philosophy of power greatly influenced Hitler and other leaders in the twentieth century who believed it was perfectly natural to amass power at both the personal and national level.

Nietzsche despised the church of his day and Christianity in general. To a certain extent, he was a completely consistent evolutionary thinker, who believed morality to be anchored in the survival of the fittest.

Consider these words from his work *The Antichrist*.

> What is good?—Whatever augments the feeling of power, the will to power, power itself, in man.
> What is evil?—Whatever springs from weakness.
> What is happiness?—The feeling that power *increases*—that resistance is overcome.
> Not contentment, but more power; *not* peace at any price, but war; *not* virtue, but efficiency (virtue in the Renaissance sense, *virtu*, virtue free of moral acid).
> The weak and the botched shall perish: first principle of *our* charity. And one should help them to it.
> What is more harmful than any vice?—Practical sympathy for the botched and the weak—Christianity....[8]

Not all Enlightenment thinkers agreed with Nietzsche's ethics, but his emphasis on power was the natural outcropping of evolutionary thinking and the failure of reason and choice to produce a life worth living.

The Christian shift toward power

One of the points we are trying to make is that the church has tended to follow the culture. When the Enlightenment said reason was supreme, the church followed. When Voluntarism said the will was supreme, the church followed. It is not surprising, therefore, that

---

[8] *The Antichrist*, translated by H. L. Mencken (New York: Alfred A. Knopf) 1918, p. 43 – https://www.gutenberg.org/files/19322/19322-h/19322-h.htm#THE_ANTICHRIST parenthetical content included in the original.

when the culture moved toward power as the key to life, the church moved in a similar direction.

Christians turned to the Holy Spirit for power to make their choices and beliefs "work." The greatest compliment you could give to a service, a sermon, or any other Christian experience was that it was "powerful." Power became the test for authentic Christian experience.

The problem here is that the model of **reason + choice** for life change was not altered. It was simply hoped that a boost of power from the Holy Spirit would make it work. Or, in another direction, it was hoped that the removal of wicked spirits would eliminate the barriers that kept it from working. The core model: **reason + choice = life change** remained the same.

The point here is not that there is anything wrong with reason, truth, will, choices, the Holy Spirit, power, or deliverance. Hopefully, we all are growing in our capacity to interact in all of these arenas. The point is that we have asked them to fill a role they were not designed to fill. We have asked them to create character change.

During my years in ministry, I (Marcus) have seen hundreds of people have profound experiences in which Jesus healed memories and removed demons. This type of spiritual power is a good thing. On the other hand, it does not, in and of itself, produce character or maturity. As Neil Anderson wrote, "There is no such thing as instant maturity, but the ability to experience your freedom in Christ can happen in a relatively short period of time."⁹

In most churches, we fail on both counts—we do not pursue the practice of spiritual power that produces freedom, and we employ a model of maturity based on the Enlightenment and Voluntarism.

Even churches that include spiritual power are simply adding it to the same Enlightenment/Voluntarist model of maturity development, hoping it will infuse the process with a power source that will finally make the model work.

The core model adopted by the church for character development does not work because we are asking truth, choice, and power to generate character change, but that is not a task they are capable of performing.

Grasping Jim's explanations of the shortcomings of the Enlightenment/Voluntarist/Power model has helped me (Marcus) understand a lot of my struggles as a Christian. It actually fits my experience perfectly.

- Truth: I am a well-educated Christian. I have memorized entire books of the Bible, mastered Greek and Hebrew, earned two masters degrees and a doctorate.

- Choice: I have struggled with all sorts of flesh problems in my life. I could never understand why trips to the altar and life management plans never seemed to produce long-term fruit.

---

9   September 29, 2014 – "Third Step In Overcoming Depression" – https://ficm.org/2014/09/?post_type=neilsblogs

- Power: I was raised in a family that practiced spiritual warfare, and I know more about it than most Christians. I have also sought the Spirit's power in many venues and with many different people.

Yet even with the Spirit and an understanding of spiritual warfare, I have struggled to make my life work in some very practical ways. One has been anxiety. A few years ago, I nearly had a breakdown as panic attacks became more frequent and anxiety settled into my body as a daily experience. It was a problem I couldn't think my way out of. I couldn't choose my way out of it. I couldn't cast out a demon and get rid of it. Believe me, I tried all of these. I had people lay hands on me with no fruit.

The reality is, I had an emotional capacity issue I am still addressing. The model of truth, choice, and power couldn't fix my problem, and there are many Christians in the same boat, trying to figure out why their Christianity doesn't work.

Conclusion

Power is an important element of the Christian life. We need the power of the Spirit's anointing to function in our calling. Spiritual power can perform miracles, bring freedom from spiritual blockages, and remove wicked spirits. But power does not produce character. It is clearly helpful to get rid of unwanted demons and to experience the healing presence of Christ in traumatic memories. But these breakthrough moments do not change our character, they merely clear the path for our character development.

The key to character change is anchored in love and relational attachment. We will explain this pathway in the final chapter. Before that, however, we need to look at the final step of the failed character-change model the church has embraced—the step of tolerance, or surrender.

6: TOLERANCE

Tolerance became the culture's top value as the Voluntarist model failed to change lives. Children raised in Christianity dropped out of church, citing the failure of older Christians to demonstrate desirable character. Rigid beliefs (truth) led to broken fellowship and too many different churches who didn't get along. Making right choices (will) was not making loving homes and marriages. In fact, many of the Christians who forced themselves to do the right thing were hard, cold, dry, and unpleasant on the inside. Affairs and child abuse continued in churches where powerful leaders and the power of the Holy Spirit (power) was praised. Christians seemed to echo Rodney King's statement during the Los Angeles riots, "Can we, can we get along?"[10]

Tolerance is a loaded word in the twenty-first century Western world, filled with political overtones. Some define it as the virtue that refuses to condemn any behavior or lifestyle as evil—except the behavior that condemns something as evil. While some Christians increasingly moralized about cultural trends, America moved in a very amoral direction called *tolerance.*

Many Christians, even those who stayed in church, became hesitant to identify with the voices proclaiming themselves to speak biblical truth, condemn bad choices, or represent special power from God and the

---

10   Rodney King video YouTube from May 1, 1992 retrieved March 29, 2018.

Holy Spirit. Shouldn't Christians be more loving and tolerant than the rest of culture? Shouldn't Christians love their neighbors?

In this book, we are proposing that tolerance, as a Christian virtue, is loving your enemies. *Tolerance* as it is being used in our culture and our churches, however, is more like giving up on the possibility of change. The modern concept of tolerance was born out of the hopelessness created by the flawed model of life change the church has championed.

> **IT IS THE INABILITY TO FIND EFFECTIVE MEANS OF CHANGE THAT HAS LED OUR CULTURE TO MAKE TOLERANCE ITS HIGHEST VALUE.**

The skewed model created in response to the Enlightenment has left the church providing solutions for change that don't work and left people believing change is impossible. Better choices empowered by the Spirit and based on the Bible have not transformed lives the way it has been advertised from pulpits and television shows.

Waving the white flag

When the only model for character change we have is anchored in truth, choice, and power—and when that model doesn't work—we either need to scrap the model or wave the white flag of surrender and embrace the fact that change is impossible.

If people cannot change sexual orientation, stay in love, avoid sexual encounters, deal with severe addictions, lose weight, stop molesting children, control their tempers (and a myriad of other issues) by 1) knowing they should not, 2) making a decision to stop, or 3) having a powerful religious experience, then tolerance is all that is left. The church has been forced in this direction by the ineffectiveness of the Voluntarist model to affect character change.

It is the inability to find effective means of change that has led our culture to make tolerance its highest value. To improve the tolerance alcoholics received and give them a chance to start again, alcoholism was reframed as a disease.

It was clear that human will (choices) did not make alcoholism go away but that some people could stop after an encounter with God's power. Then we discovered alcoholism had a genetic component, and that inflamed the fight about the will and determinism for all sorts of characteristics based on our DNA. Yet, we have discovered that with enough relational joy in their lives, even people with a genetic predisposition toward something like addictions can live out of their joy and not out of their genetics.[11]

Relational joy is a better path than tolerance, which is little more than hopelessness about change. Relational joy, however, does not flow when there is condemnation in the air. What is needed we will address in the next chapter.

The solution of choice that Christians have offered to culture and themselves (truth, choice, and power) has done little to touch character, identity, and person-

---

11   For more on this subject watch the DVDs that come with "Restarting" by Jim Wilder and Ed Khouri.

ality. As a result, most have reached the conclusion that the kindest thing to do is just accept people the way they are without any expectation of change (after all, no one seems to have a solution that works).

> **WITH ENOUGH RELATIONAL JOY IN THEIR LIVES, EVEN PEOPLE WITH A GENETIC PREDISPOSITION TOWARD ADDICTIONS CAN LIVE OUT OF THEIR JOY AND NOT OUT OF THEIR GENETICS.**

When people are having trouble getting by and facing enormous challenges because they have characteristics that are disliked, unwanted, or destructive with genetic elements, culture is now inclined to say they are just "born that way." Tolerance is better than excluding, drowning, hanging, or burning them at the stake.

If they didn't have a choice, and a powerful religious experience didn't change them, isn't Christianity out of answers?

Reinventing a more tolerant God

In a culture dominated by tolerance, it seems increasingly obvious to some that God must be tolerant in the same way the culture is.

The doctrine of hell is especially difficult to explain. Surely, a loving God would not condemn to hell people who (1) did not know the truth, (2) could not choose otherwise, or (3) lacked the mental or economic power to do the right thing. Therefore, we need God (and

Christianity) to be more tolerant and loving. Post-modern Christianity has done just that.

Many church goers reject what they see as an Old Testament God who condemns people in favor of a New Testament Jesus whose core value would be tolerance.

In the middle of the last century, a famous anthropologist[12] developed the idea that God did not make people in His own image. Rather, people created a god in their own image. Following an evolutionary model, he suggested that people noticed animals with qualities they admired and desired for themselves. Bears were strong. Foxes were shrewd. Eagles were majestic.

They began to honor these animals, and soon began to honor the spirits of these animals (thus creating totemism). Over time, the spirits of the animals became disconnected from them and were honored in their own right for the qualities they possessed as "gods." Eventually, man created one divine being who possessed all of the qualities that people longed to see in themselves, thus creating a god in their own image.

TOLERANCE IS MUCH MORE HOPELESS THAN MERCY.

We see this same pattern in the search for the historical Jesus. It has often been pointed out that when we discard the historicity of the New Testament and go looking for the historical Jesus on our own, we inevitably discover a Jesus who looks remarkably like us. Marxists found a Marxist Jesus. Feminists found a

---

12   Émile Durkheim

feminist Jesus. Others, who had rejected Jesus, found a Jesus who was easy to reject.

This tendency to create a God who looks like us can be seen in what has happened to God in our post-modern world. We have created a God who looks like us—He has no solutions for life change and simply tolerates everyone, loving them and bringing them to heaven simply because they exist. Tolerance is much more hopeless than mercy. Mercy gives people who have failed another chance by providing something they did not have before.

> **THE VOLUNTARIST MODEL PROVIDED SOLUTIONS THAT DIDN'T PRODUCE CHANGE AND THEN CONDEMNED PEOPLE TO HELL FOR NOT BEING ABLE TO CHANGE.**

The Voluntarist model embraced by the church provided solutions that didn't produce change and then condemned people to hell for not being able to change. This is so fundamentally unjust, it was only natural for people to look for a more tolerant god who did not condemn anything or anyone.

This problem of reinventing God didn't start with post-modernism. Voluntarists invented a god who condemned people for believing wrong things, making wrong choices, and failing to find his power. When the Voluntarist model didn't work, the god we had created from that model came into question.

Conclusion

Tolerance is the outcome of an Enlightenment Christianity which created solutions that do not work. The Enlightenment told Christianity that better truth, better choices, and greater power led to better human beings. The church agreed and proposed to culture that God was the one with truth, will, and power.

> **THE CHURCH NEEDS TO PROVIDE SOMETHING THE CULTURE DOESN'T HAVE.**

In this "utopia," the human will was seen to be God's agent for spiritual growth. However, something was clearly missing. In colonial Massachusetts, the state church denied baptism to the children of those who did not demonstrate Christian character. This led to a drastic decline in church attendance, and the rules quickly had to be softened.

Those who despaired of seeing character transformation due to the fallen nature of the will thought, "At least we will be saved if not changed." In America this soon degraded into a sort of "decisionism" in which a decision to accept Jesus got one into heaven even if character on earth was little changed.

American and Western Christianity lived on fighting for truth, choices, and power until culture began to lose tolerance. Failure to produce Christ-like character left Western Christianity dying on the beach like a stranded whale. At that very moment the Enlightenment made a discovery which might have rivaled the earth going around the sun.

Antonio Damasio, M.D. published *Descartes' Error: Emotion, Reason and the Human Brain* (1994). He showed that something much more basic than conscious thought determined who our brain thought we were. Damasio challenged the Enlightenment philosophers, saying they had it wrong. The secret to human nature was something more fundamental than truth, choices, power, and tolerance.

Damasio was quickly followed by Allan Schore who has gone one step further to say that humans are formed by their attachments. Who we love with attachment love has far more influence than ideas we think, choices we *will* to make, or actions we take by power. Character and identity develop from knowing (*yada*) and loving (*hesed*) another. Now, the core Western Christian understanding of human nature based on medieval psychology has to face how the brain actually works to be human.

We live at an interesting time. Culture does not yet understand the meaning of these discoveries about the brain. Culture is still trying to take tolerance to the limits, not knowing that brain science predicts a bad outcome. The church needs to provide something the culture doesn't have. We have become so culturally relevant that we have nothing to offer the culture when it comes to character transformation.

> **CULTURE IS STILL TRYING TO TAKE TOLERANCE TO THE LIMITS, NOT KNOWING THAT BRAIN SCIENCE PREDICTS A BAD OUTCOME.**

In the next chapter we will look at the solution the Enlightenment missed until now. There is a strange parallel between attachment—called *hesed* in Hebrew and *agape* in Greek—and the attachment love that forms character. We will add what Jesus said was at the heart of being His disciple to what we have discovered about the brain. We will look at the transformative solution of loving your enemies.

7: The Hesed Solution

In light of the failed model for life change that grew out of the Enlightenment, we need to ask a few questions.

- Could it be that character change has more to do with changing who we know and who we love than what we believe and how we choose to behave?

- Could it be that defective character grows out of a failure to know God or love Him deeply, rather than a lack of intellect or anointing?

- Could it be that without loving others we cannot say we love God?

- Could it be that for people to change into who God has created them to be, we must see more than their past and their actions?

- Could this mean that we develop Christ-like character by loving people who think they are our enemies?

These questions all challenge the Enlightenment-driven paradigm that **truth + choices + power = transformation**. Instead, they suggest that a paradigm based on love (specifically the biblical ideal of *hesed* love) is far more effective at producing character change than the skewed model developed in reaction to Enlightenment philosophy. This type of love should not be confused with the post-modern obsession with tolerance. It is something much deeper.

A *hesed* model of discipleship

The Hebrew word *hesed*[13] describes the core of God's character. *Hesed* has often been translated *loyalty* because it refers to a love born out of relationship or attachment. God loves us, not because we believe right things, practice good behavior, or live with power. God loves us because He is bonded to us. *Hesed* refers to the "sticky love" that stays attached regardless of how we act or what value we add.

When *hesed* replaces truth as the foundation of discipleship, the whole model self-corrects. Placing love at the core of the transformation process allows truth, choice, and power to play their proper roles and not bear a weight they were never intended to carry.

The biblical idea that *hesed* love should be the anchor of the transformation process agrees with the latest news coming from brain science. Developments in modern brain science have made it clear that any model of transformation and character change must be anchored in the development of a love bond with God and His people.

This is the goal of a *hesed* model of discipleship. We want to build joyful and transformative bonds with both God and His people through Jesus Christ, trusting

---

13   The word can also be spelled *chesed* in English because the initial *h* is guttural. We have chosen the simpler spelling because saying "hess-ed" is closer to the Hebrew than saying "chess-ed." The emphasis goes on the first syllable.

that *hesed* attachment will do more to transform character than truth, choice, and power can possibly hope to achieve without it.

D.A. Carson wrote that the church is a collection of natural enemies.[14] Most churches today seem to be more like a collection of affinity groups. Yet, the New Testament church was clearly filled with people groups who, apart from Christ, wanted nothing to do with each other. Hellenistic and Hebraic Jews didn't trust each other, but they were one in Christ. Samaritans and Gentiles were not accepted by Jewish society, but they were welcomed in Christ. "Barbarians, Scythians, slave, and free"—the church was a place where natural enemies learned to love one another. It was in loving each other and in loving God that transformation occurred. This is *hesed* discipleship.

We see the power of loving attachment to transform lives in many recovery settings. Groups established to provide "accountability" often produce bonded friendships over time. When such groups work, it is because deep attachments are formed in which "I know the

---

14   D. A. Carson, *Love in Hard Places* (Crossway, 2002) p. 61. Full quote below.
Ideally, however, the church itself is not made up of natural "friends." It is made up of natural enemies. What binds us together is not common education, common race, common income levels, common politics, common nationality, common accents, common jobs, or any-thing else of that sort. Christians come together, not because they form a natural collocation, but because they have all been saved by Jesus Christ and owe him a common allegiance. In the light of this common allegiance, in the light of the fact that they have all been loved by Jesus himself, they commit themselves to doing what he says—and he commands them to love one another. In this light, they are a band of natural enemies who love one another for Jesus' sake.

worst about you but love you too much to leave you in the mess you're in." The real power in such groups is not the accountability but the attachments that call out our true identities.

Fear bonds vs Joy bonds

As I (Marcus) reflect on my own journey, I realize I have built much of my Christianity on a fear bond with God and His people rather than a joy bond. I got saved at the age of three because I was afraid of going to hell. I bonded to God out of fear of what would happen if I didn't measure up or made a mistake so big that I missed out on His salvation.

Since I was so young when I made the decision to become a Christian (and avoid hell), there was a lot of trauma in that bond. It seemed to me that God was the sort of person who demanded to be loved or He was going to kill you. It was a little bit like He was holding a gun to my head and saying, "You better love me or else." It didn't really motivate much love, but it did create an intense desire to try. My will was fully engaged out of fear of a God I did not feel close to.

In a similar way, many of the bonds I formed with God's people were fear bonds. I learned to perform for them and act like a good Christian. But the better I got at playing the part of the devoted Christian, the more fearful I became that what I had wasn't real and that God was going to reject me in the end.

A lack of *hesed* in my walk with God and my relationships with His people left me with no other alternative than to turn to truth, choice, and power to make my Christianity work. When I did well, I felt okay about things. But on days when I struggled, everything felt hollow, and I felt like a fraud waiting to be exposed. I have found this is a sentiment shared by many Christian leaders.

My much desired transformation journey has been largely unsatisfying because it was not rooted in love, and no amount of truth, choosing, and power can create love. My growth has come from interacting with mentors, friends, and people who know me in my weakness as well as my strength.

Loving your enemies

What the church needs is a discipleship model whose goal is to produce Christians whose character is transformed so completely they aren't simply kind to their enemies by force of the will, they learn to love their enemies.

The best indicator of growing *hesed* is the increasing love for our enemies. This is very practical, because our brain easily makes enemies out of the people around us when we are hurt or afraid. It is this tendency of the brain to make enemies out of people who hurt us that lies behind every character flaw. Therefore, it stands to reason that our character flaws can only change as we learn to love our enemies.

This reality was driven home by the story of a young Christian who went to a Muslim country to share Christ in any way he could. All went well for the few weeks he was there. Several people gave their lives to Christ and many Christians were encouraged in their faith. However, as he was preparing to leave the country, he was arrested at the airport.

For the next several weeks he was beaten daily and began to sink into despair and anger. He felt abandoned by God and hated his captors. Then one day, in the midst of being beaten by his interrogator, the Holy Spirit spoke to him in a tangible way and said, "Do you have any idea how much I love this man?" As another blow struck him, he responded, "You'll have to forgive me if I don't feel the same way right now."

That night, God met the young man in his cell and gave him a peace he had never felt before. He repeated again, "I want you to love this man the way I do."

The next morning, when he entered the room where his interrogator waited, he felt an unexpected calmness. He walked toward him, looked him in the eye and said, "As long as we are going to be spending time together, we may as well be friends." Then he reached out his hand and said, "Hi, my name is Dan." The interrogator broke down and began to sob. He quickly left the room, and the young man never saw him again.

Today, Dan has moved beyond choosing to do good things for people he hates. He has learned to love his enemies, and God has taken away his fear.[15]

MERCY EXTENDS A SECOND CHANCE AND GOES THE SECOND MILE TO EXTEND THE LOVE THAT MAKES CHANGE POSSIBLE.

---

15   https://www.youtube.com/watch?v=qnpCR_aeXgU published May 4, 2011 retrieved March 29, 2018. From CBN "Imprisoned in Iran" - Dan Baumann

This young man discovered *hesed* for his captor. With *hesed* as the foundation, it was relatively easy to believe true things, make good choices, and experience God's power. If the order was reversed, however, believing true ideas, making good choices, and experiencing God's power was not going to produce *hesed* for his captors.

Bandits, Bullets, and the Gospel

It was a dark, cloudy night in the hamlet of Rio Negro, accessible only by horses in the Andes Mountains. Don Pastor Muñoz had befriended the local people and protected them from being exploited so, in time, his home became a local church. Don Pastor invited Jim's parents to come and teach.

Although there was no electricity, the Wilders had a filmstrip projector that worked off of a flame. People gathered from across the mountains to see this wonder, and, soon, there were far too many to fit in the house. They took the projector outside, using the whitewashed wall as a screen. Although they could not be seen, the hillsides on both sides of the house were soon filled with people.

This remote mountain region was not simply the home of the indigenous people Don Pastor befriended. It was also a great place for the marauding bandits from the valleys below to hide from the law. Who should show up for the filmstrip show on the life of St. Paul but the leader of the biggest band of bandits and his "boys" all armed to the teeth! Jim, being a small boy, could see up under the ponchos where the belts of ammunition and hand grenades hung out of sight of the adults.

The army also knew the bandits hid in these mountains. Because the nights were long, the army commander decided it would be great to see the local entertainment, and he and his whole company arrived for the program. They also took the precaution to arrive fully armed. The soldier's arms, ammunition, and grenades were out for anyone to see.

Knowing a fierce firefight would break out if these two groups discovered the other was there, the local Christians provided hospitality for each group on opposing hillsides while the Christians all sat in the middle between the two.

Jim's father showed the filmstrip and explained about the Christian life to the whole group while being careful not to invite interested individuals to come forward. After the program was done, Jim's father and the local leaders offered the soldiers and bandits a chance to receive a personal visit and sent them home by different paths. The Christians were there to love them all but could easily be killed by one side for loving the other.

Persecution

The Bible school where Jim spent much of his youth included students who had previously been bandits or vigilantes who killed any Christians in the region. There were some rough characters in that Bible school. As with many gangs, if a gangster became a Christian, that person was marked for death by his former associates. No rural family could safely hide the convert for fear of being killed as well, so the Christians in the cities gave them shelter.

Much like the case of Saul of Tarsus who persecuted the church, these enemies were the reason Jim's family was there. Loving these enemies was the purpose of the mission. In addition, there was a sort of relationship between killing Christians and conversion. Watching how Christians died or acted when threatened with torture and death resulted in more than one conversion. Jim says, "That meant that the person who hours ago was killing us now needed our refuge and care lest he be killed." Was this a setup or real? Who could tell? What was clear was the reality that if Christians did not love their enemies, there would be no transformation of souls.

Boys with rocks

When Jim was about seven years old, his family lived in a town where they walked to church. On the way, they were frequently followed by young boys shouting insults. The family simply ignored the insults and walked on to church. One Sunday, as they crossed the bridge, the boy following them began throwing small rocks, so the family turned briefly as the boy ran off.

"Did you see what house that boy came out of?" Jim's mother asked him. Jim pointed out the house. He had been in trouble with his mother for throwing rocks a few times himself. Now he was going to see what would happen to the little tormenter!

"Remember that house," Mother said. "Next week, when we come back, we will bring him and his family a present and invite them to church. What do you think we should bring?"

Jim was dumbfounded, not because he had trouble picking gifts for people (which he does) but because of the dramatic difference in the way he was being asked to think about his enemies. This sudden change in point of view made his mind spin.

What he had failed to realize in Rio Negro between the bandits and the army and had missed with the converted persecutors in Bible school became a personal reality for his character when facing a boy with rocks. Jim wanted to throw bigger rocks back. But, loving our enemies does not have to wait for persecution to start. Almost any little boy or girl can reveal the change we need if we are to be like Christ.

Our change is not forced by willpower. Rather, we are constrained by the love of Christ,[16] for it is this *hesed* love that did not let us go even when we were still enemies of God. Without *hesed* love, all our spiritual power is noise.[17]

Is this love from Christ only a truth to believe? Is it the sort of choice we make when we don't feel like we care for someone in the slightest? Is *hesed* love something that lets us walk away from a boy with stones or something that brings us back to his house with gifts?

Hesed is something that is developed through interaction with others. We love God because He first loved us[18]—and while we were yet sinners and enemies no less! Could this attachment love of God actually be the key to developing Christ-like character?

16	2 Corinthians 5:14
17	1 Corinthians 13
18	1 John 4:19

Hesed love is grown as we experience it from others and "pay it forward." This is how it grows in us and becomes contagious in others. It starts with God's unconditional *hesed* love and moves forward as our hearts are changed by that love.

Looking at the brain once more

The 1990s became the "decade of the brain" when brain scans of living organs replaced the study of dead brains. Now people could watch what grew, responded, and changed in living beings. The study of brain scans quickly revealed that the human identity formed as a strong response to whoever the baby attached to in the first years of life.

In many different ways, the interaction between a baby and the attachment figure duplicated the key human features in the baby's brain. While genetics created options, the patterns that developed were learned by the baby through relational practice motivated by the desire for joy and peaceful connections. Joyful attachment love is the secret center to all desirable human traits.

After puberty, the human brain expands its attachment to a larger group of people (peers) who also shape personality and character profoundly. In every case of positive character change, there are important attachments to others. These attachment centers in the brain remain active when we are asleep, passed out, under the influence of drugs, distracted, unfocused, and paying no attention to them at all. The attachment systems stay on whether we are motivated or not.

Attachment runs whether we are making choices or drifting. Attachment pays little attention to what we prefer or how much power we feel we have. Quite to the contrary, the attachment systems in the brain direct what we prefer, how motivated we feel, and what choices we consider important.

Conclusion

Who you are attached to has shaped the language you speak, the country you call your own, the clothes you wear, the style of your hair, the activities you attend, the languages you learned, the places you stay, the church you attend, the foods you like, the places you shop, the phone calls you make, the vacations you take, the music you prefer, the people you consider marrying, the pets you want, the places you would like to live, and the list goes on.

We have all watched others make illogical decisions for love. We have seen people fight hard with all their will and lose to love. We have seen powerful people go down before love. We have tolerated and watched others tolerate stuff they would never have chosen but for love. Could it be that the key to the human soul is found in our attachments? Are we most profoundly shaped by who loves us, and so we attach to them as brain science now says?

If so we should expect God to say things like, "You shall love the Lord your God with all your heart, with all your soul, and with all your strength," and make that a central teaching for all God's people.

This short book does not purport to cover all the history or details of human thought for the last 500 years, all the history of the church in Western culture, the expanse of theological and philosophical discussion, or a complete review of what the Bible says about God and humans.

Rather than relying on "bulletproof truth," the solution of choice, or a more powerful presentation, we ask you to see for yourself whether God's *hesed* love is central to all good things. Test for yourself whether every place where Christians show the character of Christ isn't the result of *hesed*.

Is your heart drawn toward a love that even your enemies cannot stop?

For years I (Marcus) have been told that love is a choice. The implication was that I needed to choose the right behavior regardless of how hostile I felt inside. *Hesed* calls for something more than this. It calls for authentic attachments to be formed even with people who may be actively persecuting me or treating me with evil intent.

As the church moves forward, we need to develop discipleship agendas that are actively focused on building this Christ-like love in our attachments with one another and not simply in the choices we make despite our underlying resentments. The paradigm for change got skewed when truth replaced *hesed* love as the centerpiece of the faith. It is time for the church to change the paradigm.

Not only will it help us to take the lead in our culture rather than once again playing "follow the leader," it will also help us generate genuine life transformation.

Dr. E. James Wilder

Jim Wilder (PhD, Clinical Psychology, and MA, Theology, Fuller Theological Seminary) has been training leaders and counselors for over twenty-nine years on five continents. He is the author of ten books with a strong focus on maturity and relationship skills for leaders. His coauthored book *Living from the Heart Jesus Gave You* has sold over 100,000 copies in eleven languages. Wilder has published numerous articles and developed four sets of video and relational leadership training called THRIVE.

He has extensive clinical counseling experience and is currently executive director of Shepherd's House Inc., a nonprofit working at the intersection of brain science and theology. He is also the lead developer of the Life Model, which is building contagiously healthy Christian communities through equipping existing networks with the skills to thrive.

DR. MARCUS WARNER

Marcus Warner (MDiv, ThM, and DMin, Trinity Evangelical Divinity School) is the president of Deeper Walk International. He is a former pastor and college professor who has written several books on topics ranging from how to study the Bible to spiritual warfare, emotional healing, and leadership. Marcus has done training events for organizations such as Navigators, Willow Creek Prison Ministry, and The Moody Church. He has traveled the world with Deeper Walk equiping people on the front lines of ministry with practical tools for dealing with root issues that keep people and ministries stuck and unable to go deeepr into what God has for them.

Deeper Walk International is a 501(C)(3) nonprofit bringing together biblically-balanced teaching on emotional healing and spiritual warfare that helps people who feel stuck break through to new levels of freedom in their walk with God.

We teach about God's grace, life in the Spirit, spiritual warfare, and authentic community. What sets our training apart is how we bring it all together, then make it simple and transferable, so that people understand what it takes to walk in freedom and grow in maturity. We call this approach to ministry "heart-focused discipleship." Find us at DeeperWalkInternational.org.

Life Model Works is a 501(C)(3) nonprofit leading the way in refining the process of transformation into the image of Christ and rallying others to do the same. At the heart of their efforts is the Life Model: a multi-generational model of redemption and maturity from birth to death. It is based on a biblical worldview which incorporates the latest in brain science and effectively provides lasting transformation of identity, character, and culture.

The Life Model's three distinct elements are a multi-generational community, an Immanuel Lifestyle, and nineteen relational brain skills. Discover how the model can produce lasting transformation into the character of Christ at LifeModelWorks.org.